Crop Duster Pete

Peter Schellenberger

ISBN 979-8-88832-268-0 (paperback)
ISBN 979-8-88832-269-7 (digital)

Copyright © 2023 by Peter Schellenberger

All rights reserved. No part of this publication may be reproduced, distributed, or transmitted in any form or by any means, including photocopying, recording, or other electronic or mechanical methods without the prior written permission of the publisher. For permission requests, solicit the publisher via the address below.

Christian Faith Publishing
832 Park Avenue
Meadville, PA 16335
www.christianfaithpublishing.com

Printed in the United States of America

In loving memory of Tracy Bevill.

Hello, I'm Crop Duster Pete. I fly an airplane to help farmers protect their crops. Come along with me on this adventure.

Ring, ring! It's five in the morning. Time to get up. Let's hurry! Let's throw on some clothes, I'll snatch up my flight bag and flight suit, and I'm off to fly.

Here we are at the flying service. That's the ground crew getting our airplane ready for the busy day ahead. They have already pulled the plane out of the hangar and are filling it with fuel and cleaning the windows.

Let's head into the office to pick up our maps. These maps show us where the fields are that need to be sprayed.

Praire Ag

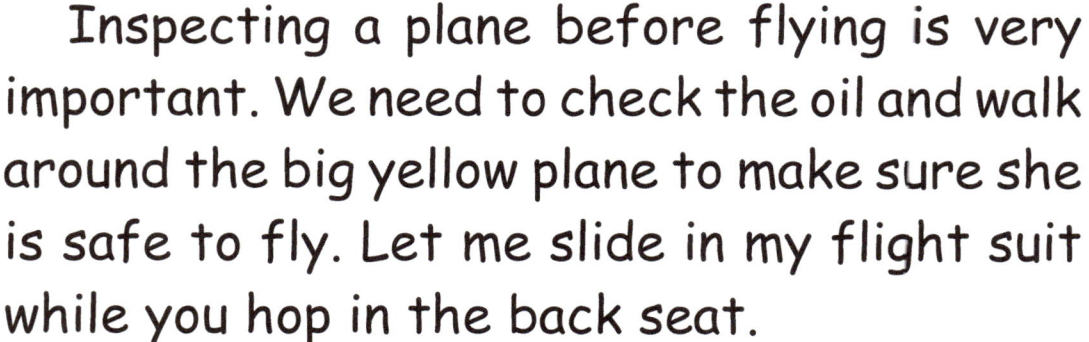

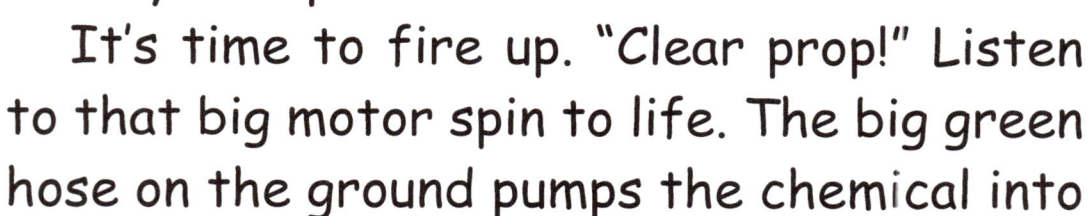

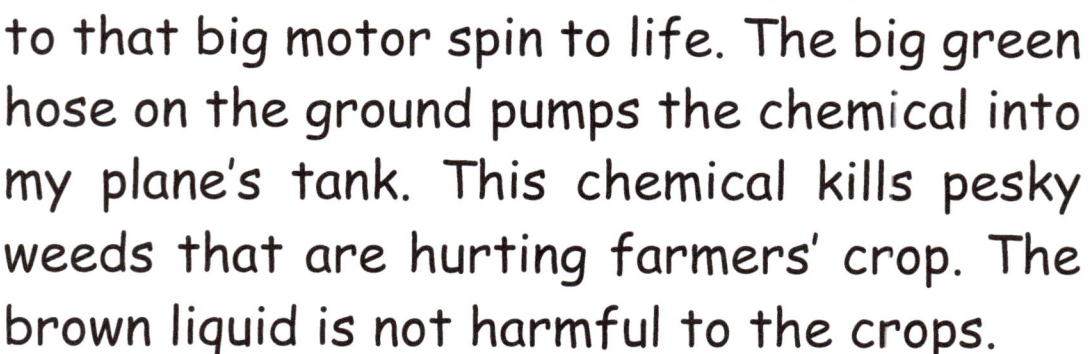

Inspecting a plane before flying is very important. We need to check the oil and walk around the big yellow plane to make sure she is safe to fly. Let me slide in my flight suit while you hop in the back seat.

It's time to fire up. "Clear prop!" Listen to that big motor spin to life. The big green hose on the ground pumps the chemical into my plane's tank. This chemical kills pesky weeds that are hurting farmers' crop. The brown liquid is not harmful to the crops.

6

The tank is full. Let's put on our helmets so we don't bonk our heads. I will say a little prayer and then we'll take off down the runway.

Here we go! Now that we're in the air, I'm going to point us toward our field.

There it is. We've made it to our field. I'm going to look for power lines or trees that will be in the way.

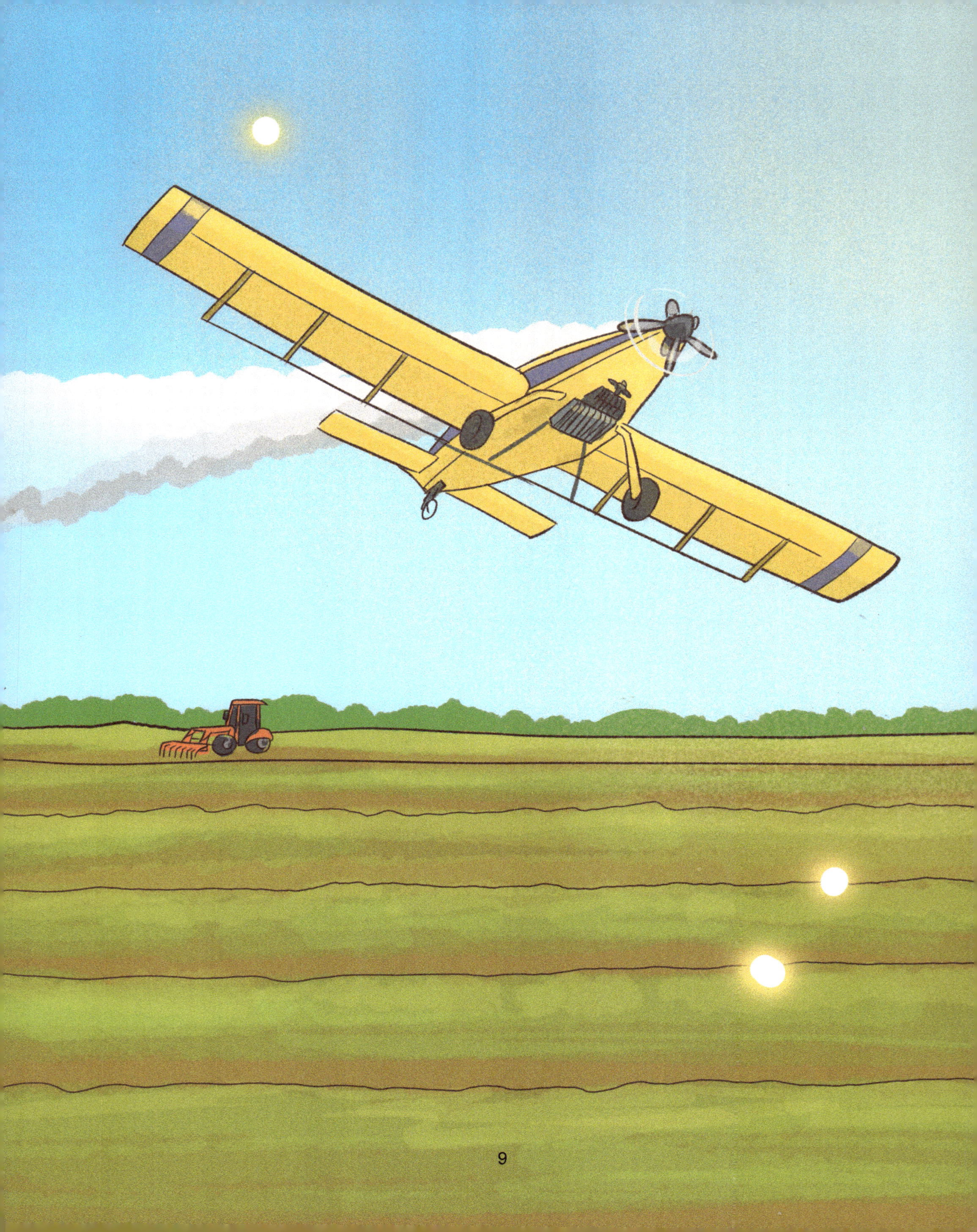

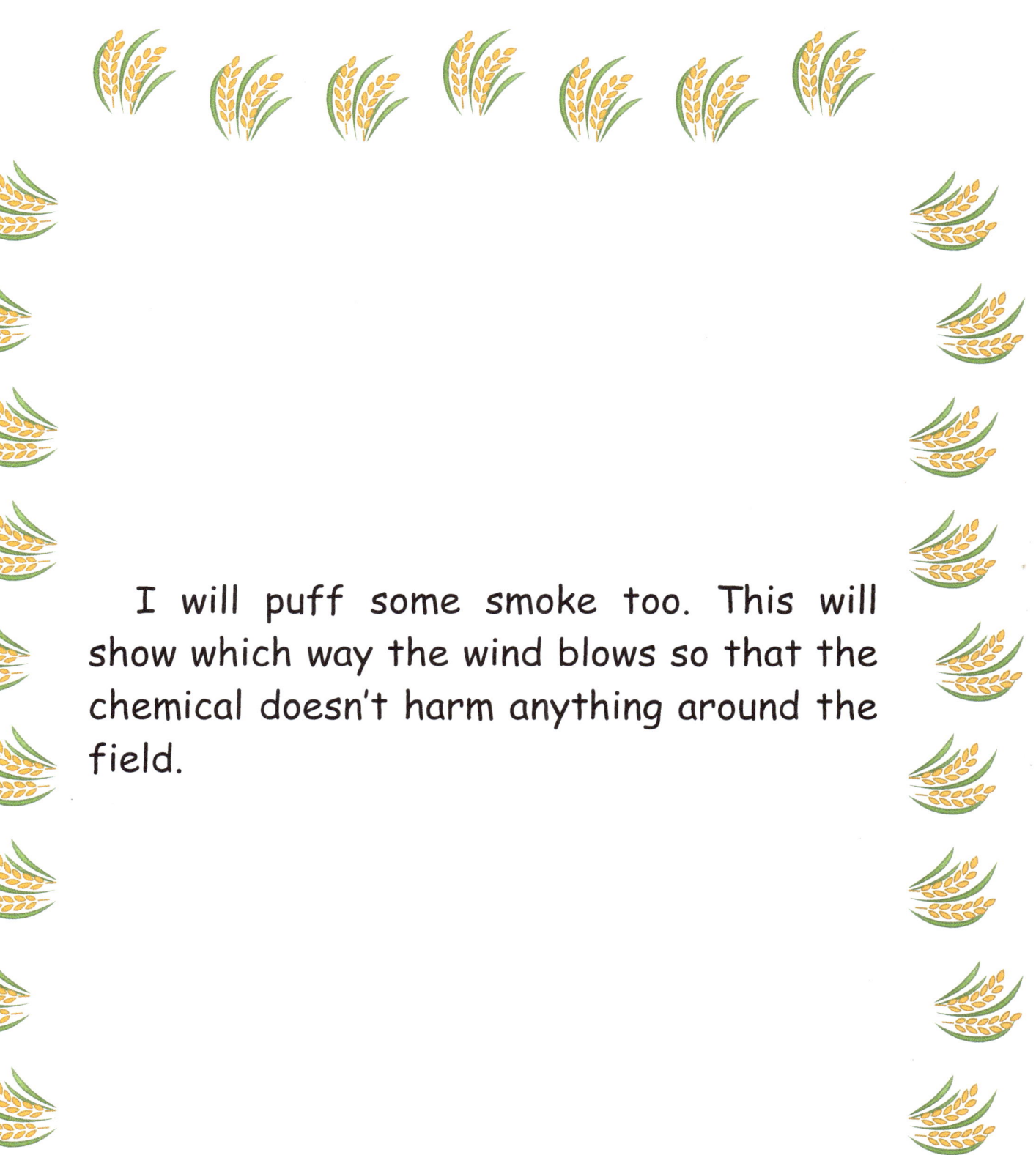

I will puff some smoke too. This will show which way the wind blows so that the chemical doesn't harm anything around the field.

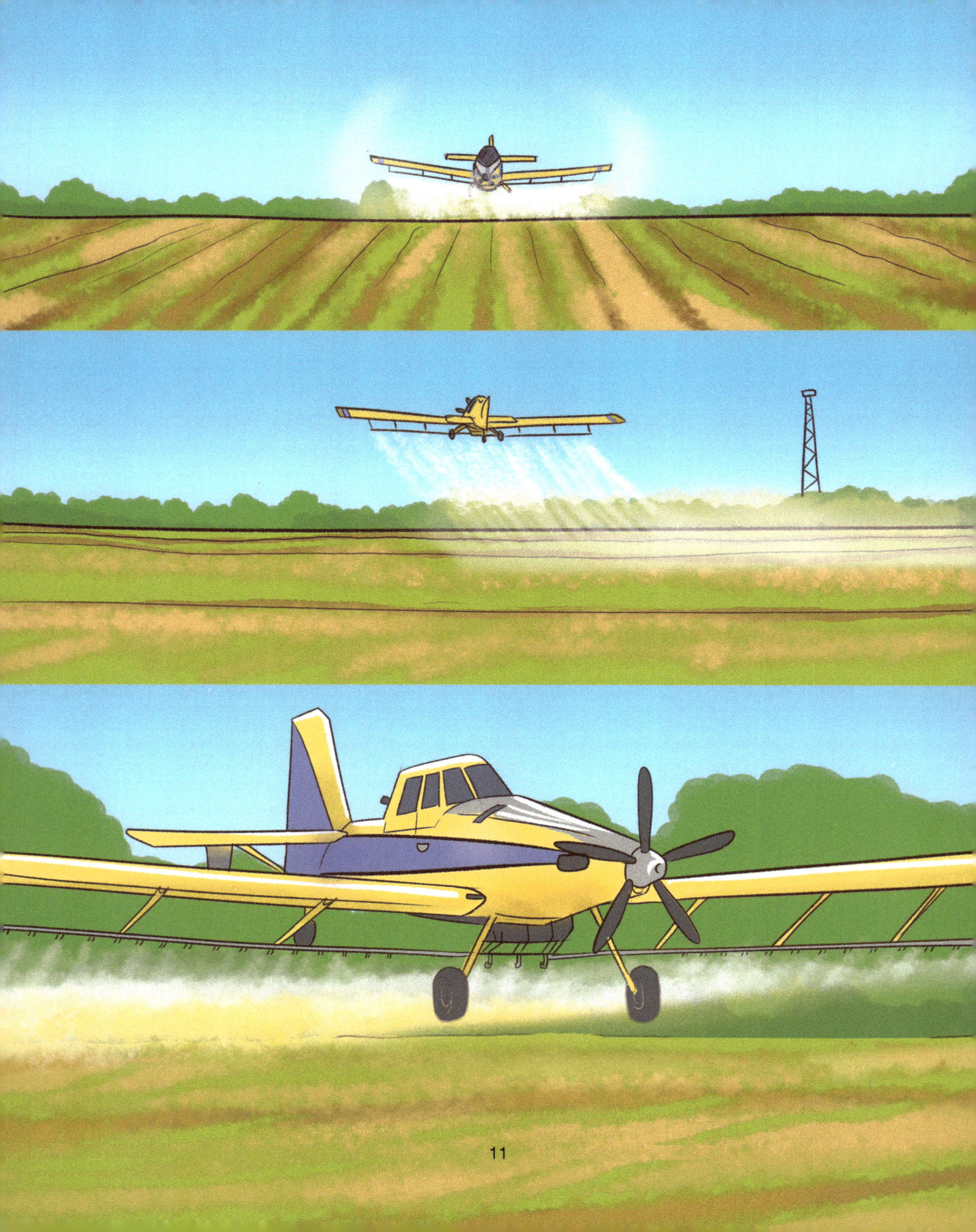

Everything looks safe. I'll line up the plane on the field and dive in. Hammer down, it's time to have some fun. Back and forth, up and down, we're working our way across the field.

13

The tank is emptied out, so we have to land to grab another load.

There are a lot of fields to be sprayed today, so let's keep moving quickly but safely.

Field after field we get the work done until it's time to make one final landing.

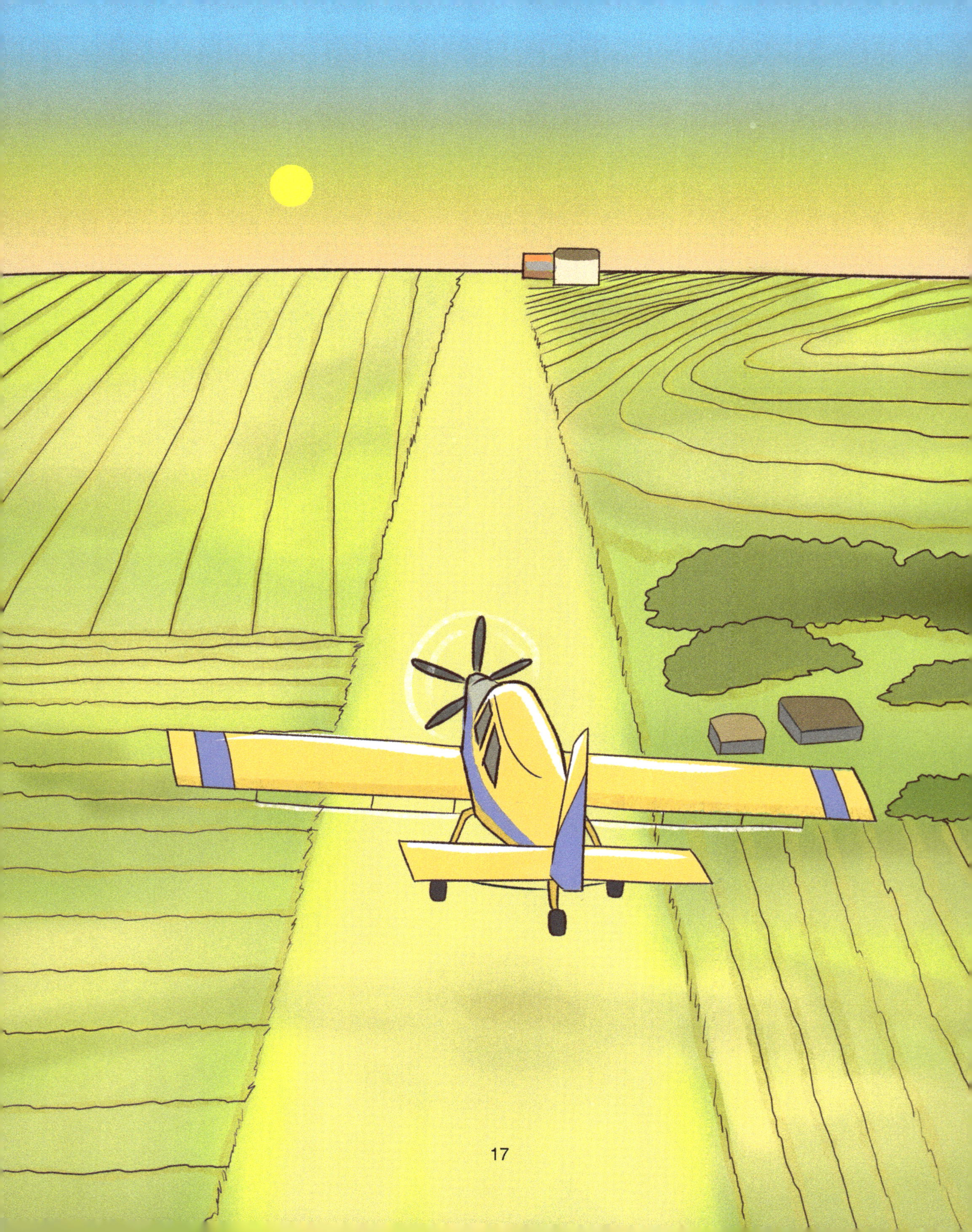

Errch! The tires touch. We're safe on the ground once again.

It's time to wash the plane and put her away for the night. Then off to the house I go.

20

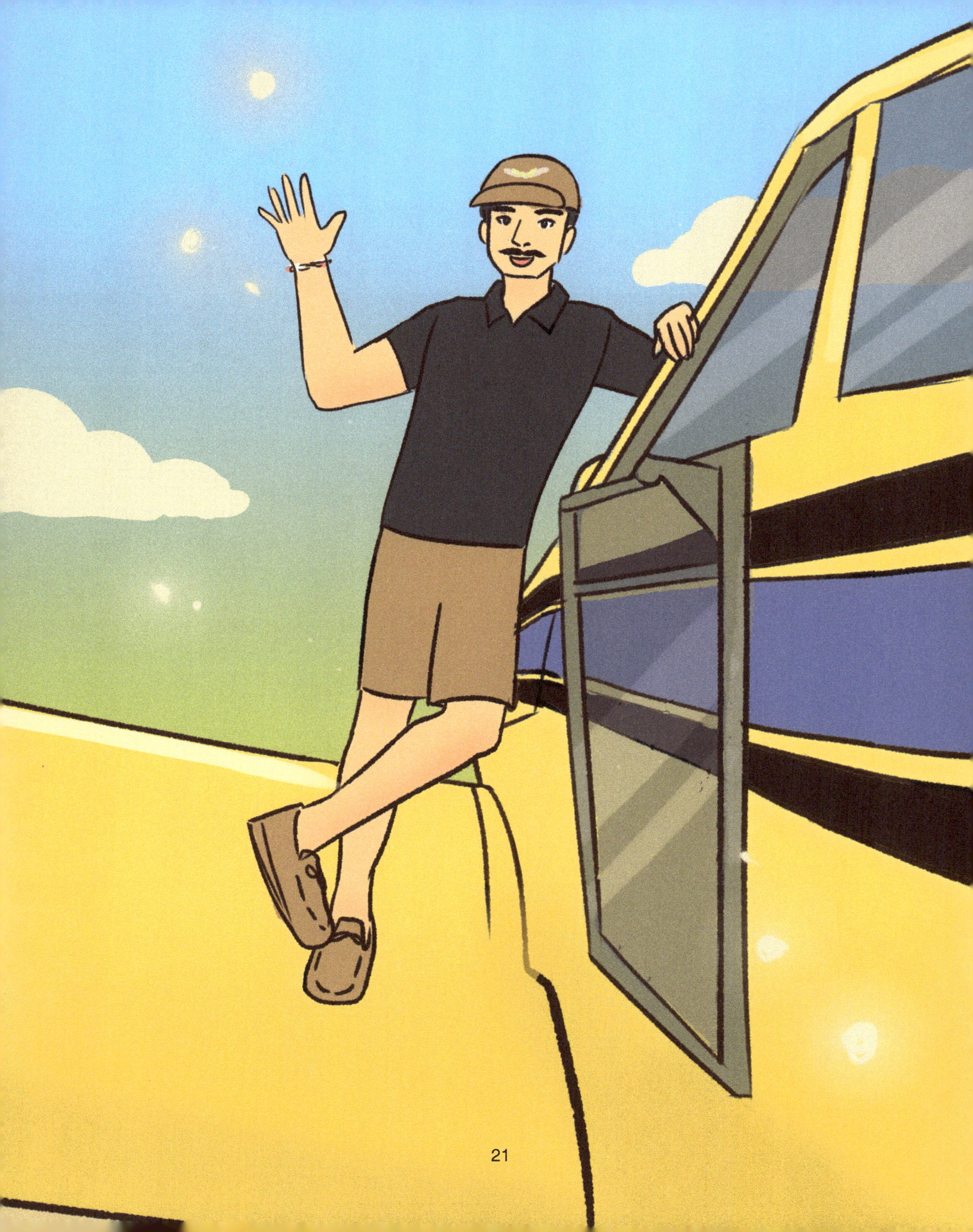

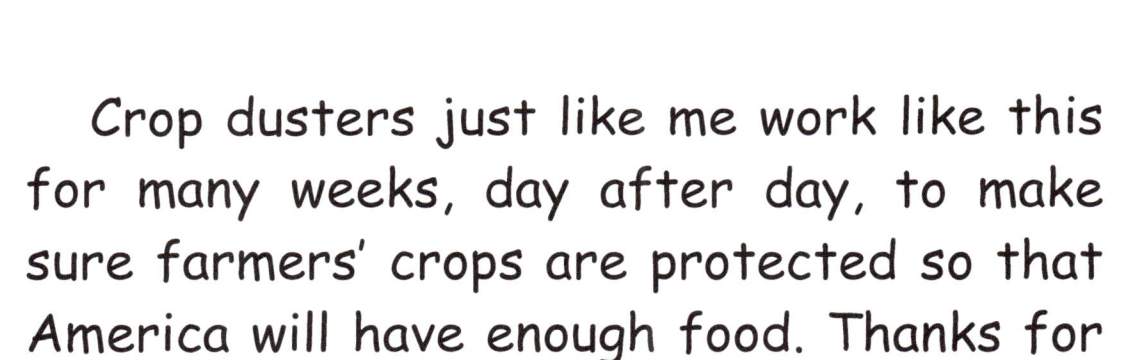

Crop dusters just like me work like this for many weeks, day after day, to make sure farmers' crops are protected so that America will have enough food. Thanks for coming with me today! See you next time.

About the Author

A third-generation pilot, Peter got the flying bug as a young boy. His love and passion for aviation have allowed him to fly in seventeen different states during his career of aerial application, firebombing, and flight instructing. He wrote *Crop Duster Pete* to inform the public on the importance and environmental safety aerial application plays in food production.

When not in the airplane, Peter enjoys running his digital marketing company, truck driving, and farming. He resides in Central Arkansas with his wife and three sons.

CPSIA information can be obtained
at www.ICGtesting.com
Printed in the USA
BVHW010520060723
666786BV00018B/752